CREATE YOUR ME MOVEMENT

CREATE YOUR ME MOVEMENT

AN EMPOWERING GUIDED JOURNAL FOR GIRLS

PATRICIA WOOSTER

ROCK
POINT

Inspiring | Educating | Creating | Entertaining

Brimming with creative inspiration, how-to projects, and useful information to enrich your everyday life, Quarto Knows is a favorite destination for those pursuing their interests and passions. Visit our site and dig deeper with our books into your area of interest: Quarto Creates, Quarto Cooks, Quarto Homes, Quarto Lives, Quarto Drives, Quarto Explores, Quarto Gifts, or Quarto Kids.

© 2018 by Patricia Wooster

First published in 2018 by Rock Point,
an imprint of The Quarto Group
142 West 36th Street, 4th Floor
New York, NY 10018 USA
T (212) 779-4972 F (212) 779-6058
www.QuartoKnows.com

Rock Point < titles are also available at discount for retail, wholesale, promotional, and bulk purchase. For details, contact the Special Sales Manager by email at specialsales@quarto.com or by mail at The Quarto Group, Attn: Special Sales Manager, 401 Second Avenue North, Suite 310, Minneapolis, MN 55401, USA.

10 9 8 7 6 5 4 3 2 1

ISBN: 978-1-63106-493-7

Editorial Director: Rage Kindelsperger
Managing Editor: Erin Canning
Associate Editor: Keyla Hernández
Cover and Interior Design: Kate Smith
Design Manager: Philip Buchanan

Printed in China

INTRODUCTION

Have you ever felt stressed, overworked, or burned out? Disconnected from your friends and family? Or wished you could achieve a certain goal but just can't figure out how to get there? Maybe you are searching for passion and purpose in life. **Maybe you are looking for CHANGE.**

Nothing promotes change better than a social movement. A social movement is when a group of people with a common cause create change. Social movements have accomplished so much in our history — they've fought injustice, brought attention to social issues, helped to preserve the environment, and stood up for what's right. With social media, it's easier than ever before to take an active part in a cause you are passionate about.

In this journal, **YOU are going to start a social movement — a ME Movement where YOU are the cause.** The goal of the ME Movement is to inspire you, to develop your purpose, to ignite your spirit, and to encourage you to get out and play. This journal will guide your ME Movement over the next twelve months, focusing on four key parts of your life:

- **PLAY:** activities that bring you happiness
- **SPIRITUALITY:** your connection to the world around you
- **STRENGTH:** your courage to handle challenges
- **PURPOSE:** what gives your life meaning

The journal includes weekly activities based on the guiding principles of a successful social movement. You will be asked to mobilize resources by identifying your talents and strong personality traits. By investing time, you will build a solid foundation for your movement to grow. And by learning to advocate, you will give rise to your own powerful voice. Your ME Movement will help you **identify positive and rewarding relationships in your life.**

This is your year of ME. Growth won't come from standing still, but from small steps that lead you to your highest self. Your ME Movement will help you to develop a set of tools to handle life's challenges. To find direction when you feel off track. To get to know yourself better. To create plans for your future. It will require some time and thinking on your part,

but you'll be rewarded with increased inspiration and greater control over your life.
Get ready to take action. Your ME Movement is just getting started!

HOW TO USE THIS JOURNAL

Your Strategy, Your Movement

- This journal is set up to inspire you in four important parts of your life:
  Play, Spirituality, Strength, and Purpose.

- Start from the beginning or skip around based on your mood! **You get to dictate your ME Movement.**

- Take the quizzes. They will help you gauge where you are in your ME Movement. Do you need a new strategy? More resources? Some outside help? Answer a few questions and find out. Doodle, draw pictures, write outside the lines. **This is your journal to personalize.**

- Use gel pens, washi tape, markers, or a regular old pen — whatever allows you to **express yourself** best.

Weekly Terminology

Each weekly exercise starts by asking you to identify a BEAUTIFUL THING and a WEEKLY #HASHTAG. Your **BEAUTIFUL THING is an opportunity to look back, express gratitude, and focus on the positive moments.** Have you had a difficult week? Your BEAUTIFUL THING will help you see some good when things are tough. Go back and read your weekly BEAUTIFUL THINGS whenever you need an extra pick-me-up.

The **WEEKLY #HASHTAG is your mantra or inspiring chant for the week** and an opportunity to look forward. Mantras are powerful because they help to focus the mind on a specific goal while getting rid of distracting thoughts. Your WEEKLY #HASHTAG can be something basic like #DOHOMEWORK or more challenging like #ONLYKINDNESS. Repeat it throughout the week and see how your mind shifts to just that one thought.

BEGIN
YOUR ME
MOVEMENT

PLAY

Do you remember the long summer days of bicycles, popsicles, and sprinklers? Maybe you created dances, wore costumes, and put on performances. Or maybe you were a regular at playing kickball, four square, and tag. No matter how you spent your time, you can probably remember a ton of moments when you experienced the pure joy and laughter that comes with play.

Keep an open mind to the following statement: **You need to keep playing for the rest of your life.** Now you may be thinking, I don't have time to play. I have homework, family obligations, and a social life. I'm not interested in revisiting my childhood right now. I've got things to do.

Play is anything but trivial. It is energizing and rejuvenating. It helps you to unwind, relax, and clear your mind. It allows you to test new ideas and tap into your imagination. Your creativity flows when you stop worrying about performance and concentrate on having a good time.

You are playing when you hang out with your friends, listen to music, or go to the movies. Build up your "play" activities by making a list of everything you enjoy doing, such as sports, art, exploring new places, or playing games. Now add a bunch of new things you want to try, so you **never run out of playful ideas.**

For the next 13 weeks, focus on rejuvenation and fun. Let your imagination run wild and be open to new possibilities. Your greatest ME Movement ideas may come when you **give yourself the freedom to PLAY.**

TEST YOUR PLAY IQ

Answer True or False for the following:

- I danced, sang, or listened to music this week. ☑T ☐ F

- I participate in creative hobbies like drawing, building, or singing. ☑T ☐ F

- I have a physical activity I do for fun. ☑T ☐ F

- I spend time using my imagination. ☑T ☐ F

- I have an activity that makes me lose track of time. ☐ T ☑F

- I am open to trying new activities. ☑T ☐ F

- I do activities to help me relax. ☑T ☐ F

- I know how I would spend an entire day to myself. ☑T ☐ F

- I don't worry about looking silly when trying something new. ☑T ☐ F

- I can quickly name three things I like to do. ☑ T ☐ F

How did you do? Commit to making every "false" answer "true" by the end of the next 13 weeks. Not using this book in order? Then pick the statements where you answered "false" and start making them come true. Have fun raising your PLAY IQ!

TURN IT UP!

ONE OF MY FAVORITE THINGS TO DO IS TO PLAY MUSIC REALLY LOUD AND DANCE MY BUTT OFF IN THE MORNING. I'LL DO IT ALONE IN MY APARTMENT. YOU CAN'T HAVE A BAD DAY AFTER THAT.

— Allison Williams, actress

What songs bring you **joy,** remind you of
your **childhood,** or make you **laugh?**
Create an official "Play" playlist of these tunes.

Beautiful Thing: _____ # _____

A CREATIVE LIFE

TAKE NOTE
OF ALL THE
GOOD THINGS
PEOPLE
ARE SAYING!

— Beth Reekles, youth author

Design a reality show around your **life.**
What would the **highlights** be? What would be some
positive things people would say about it?

Beautiful Thing: _____ # _____

SAY YES!

IF YOU GO AROUND
BEING AFRAID,
YOU'RE NEVER GOING
TO ENJOY LIFE.
YOU ONLY HAVE
ONE CHANCE,
SO YOU'VE GOT
TO HAVE FUN.

— Lindsey Vonn, ski racer

**When have you said no to doing
something fun when you should have said yes?**

I have said yes to going
outside on my trampoline
when I said no, I want
to play video games

FREED UP

I WANT TO BE A RENAISSANCE WOMAN. I WANT TO PAINT, AND I WANT TO WRITE, AND I WANT TO ACT, AND I JUST WANT TO DO EVERYTHING.

— Emma Watson, actress

If you had an entire Saturday all to yourself with no obligations, what would you do?

I would eat and go out to my fort. I would play fortnight and go out to my bar and watch videos

TAKE A LOOK

NOT LOOKING LIKE ANYONE ELSE HAS MADE THINGS EASIER FOR ME, BECAUSE I'M DISTINCTIVE.

— Rebel Wilson, actress

Look in the mirror. Write down **everything** you see that you **like** about yourself. What do you think makes you **different?** What do you like most about your "differences"?

SO FUNNY

I'M NOT LIKE THE COOL GIRLS— I'M THE OTHER GIRL. THE ONE THAT'S BASICALLY A NERD, BUT PROUD OF THAT.

— Lele Pons, internet star

What makes you **proud** about yourself?
What makes you **laugh out-loud?**

Beautiful Thing: _____ # _____

LOVE 'EM OR LEAVE 'EM

IF YOU'RE NOT HAVING A GREAT TIME AND LOVING IT STILL, THEN YOU SHOULD DO SOMETHING ELSE.

— Elle Fanning, actress

Name five activities you do but **dislike.**
And then name five activities
that sound **fun** but you've never tried.

Beautiful Thing: _____ # _____

OPEN ROAD

I THINK THERE'S A LOT TO BE SAID FOR THE HUMAN IMAGINATION. WE SPEND A LOT OF OUR LIVES JUST DAYDREAMING AND THINKING ABOUT THINGS.

— Nina Freeman, game designer

Use your **imagination** and create the
road trip of a lifetime. Where would you **go**
and what would you **see?**

Beautiful Thing: _____ # _____

FINANCIAL FREEDOM

MY GOAL ISN'T TO CHANGE THE WORLD. I JUST HOPE TO CHANGE THE PEOPLE WHO LIVE IN IT.

— Amanda Southworth, youth app developer

You're given **$1 million** to spend in a weekend.
You can **give** 25 percent to charity and
can't acquire any new things. How will you **spend** it?

Beautiful Thing: _____ # _____

EXPRESS YOURSELF

PEOPLE EXPECT YOU TO BE DOING SOMETHING COOL ALL THE TIME. IN A NORMAL LIFE, THAT'S NOT HAPPENING!

— Kaia Gerber, model

Think about a cool new **project** you can
do to liven up your day.
Create your to-do list to get your **started.**

Beautiful Thing: _____ # _____

CHILL OUT

I'M ATTRACTED TO THINGS THAT ARE IN DIRECT OPPOSITION TO SOMETHING THAT I'VE JUST DONE.

— Anna Kendrick, actress

What activities can you do to **unwind**
after a **stressful** week at school or with friends?

Beautiful Thing: _____   # _____

LEND A HAND

STEP IS LIFE. IT TAUGHT ME DISCIPLINE, TEAMWORK, HOW TO LOVE, AND HOW TO BE A GOOD TEAM.

— Blessin Giraldo, step dancer

What's something **fun**
you can do for **someone** else?

Beautiful Thing: _____ # _____

PRIORITIZE

ANY PROBLEM, BIG OR SMALL, IS PERFECT FOR YOU AS LONG AS YOU HAVE THE DRIVE TO SOLVE IT.

— Allie Weber, youth inventor

You can take seven **items** and two **people** to
a deserted island. Who and what would you **choose?**

Beautiful Thing: _____ # _____

Have you ever wondered what it means to be mindful? Or what it means to be a spiritual person? Maybe the first thing that comes to mind is religion or a person's faith. Or perhaps it makes you think of someone sitting in a yoga pose with their eyes closed in deep meditation. Spirituality is often misunderstood. There are so many definitions of it floating around, it's no wonder it can be kind of confusing.

Spirituality is about the meaning of life and your connection to the world around you. How you practice it is up to you. You can start by identifying what's important to you, and then figure out how to relate it to something bigger. It sounds kind of deep and complicated, but it's actually quite simple.

Close your eyes and imagine all of the wonderful things you want to happen in your life. Next, think about all of the good things you can do to help other people. Picture all of them coming true. Do you feel inspired? Congratulations! You just had a spiritual moment.

When you focus on positive things, it feels good. You can take a walk and experience nature and feel spiritual. **Spirituality is about bringing a sense of calm and peace into your life.** You are also practicing spirituality when you express gratitude for the good things in your life. You can do so privately in a journal, or you can share your thoughts with someone you appreciate.

These next 13 weeks will help you dig deep and grow your inner light. Look for the positive in everything you see. **When you feel happy on the inside, it shows on the outside.** You will find that your ME Movement is bursting with inspiration!

SPIRITUALITY

TEST YOUR SPIRITUALITY IQ

Answer True or False for the following:

- I purposely take moments to be alone with my thoughts. ☐ T ☐ F

- I can find the silver lining in most situations. ☐ T ☐ F

- I don't hold on to negative thoughts for very long. ☐ T ☐ F

- I like to give to people, even if I won't get anything in return. ☐ T ☐ F

- I see beauty everywhere. ☐ T ☐ F

- I don't judge other people. ☐ T ☐ F

- I tell my friends how much I appreciate them. ☐ T ☐ F

- I focus my thoughts on what I want to achieve in life. ☐ T ☐ F

- I like to focus on things outside of myself. ☐ T ☐ F

- I'm amazed by the size of the universe. ☐ T ☐ F

How's your spiritual vibe? Your "true" answers show how connected you are to the world around you. These next 13 weeks will build on that inspiration. So, go with the flow, and be prepared to raise your SPIRITUALITY IQ!

ALL YOU NEED
TO DO IS HELP
ONE PERSON,
EXPECTING
NOTHING
IN RETURN.

—Rihanna, singer

GIVING

Week 14

SPIRITUALITY

Practice **self-gratitude.**
Write a **thank-you** note to yourself
for all of the **good** stuff that
happened this week.

I HAVE TWO HANDS:
ONE FOR ME,
ONE FOR
OTHER PEOPLE.

— Millie Bobby Brown, actress

HELPING HANDS

Week 15

Beautiful Thing: _____ # _____

What have you done to **help** another person?
Did you **gain** anything from
this experience?

TODAY I KNOW THAT THERE IS STILL WORK TO BE DONE, BUT ALONG THE WAY I AM ACHIEVING MY DREAMS.

— Candace Parker, WNBA athlete

THROUGH THE AGES

Week 16

SPIRITUALITY

What are your some of your **past** dreams?
What dreams do you see having for
yourself in the **future?** If you could time
travel to the past or future, what
time period would you **choose?**

WRITE DOWN EVERYTHING YOU CAN THINK OF, NO MATTER HOW STUPID IT SEEMS.

— Daya, singer

DEEP THOUGHTS

Week 17

SPIRITUALITY

Set a timer for five minutes,
close your eyes, and **meditate** in complete
silence. Then write down your **thoughts**
and what they **mean.**

IT'S EXCITING TO SEE THAT I CAN BE WHO I AM AND PEOPLE WILL STILL GRAVITATE TOWARDS THAT.

— Yara Shahidi, actress

MY LIFE IN FILM

Week 18

Beautiful Thing: _____ # _____

Which **movies** best represent **you** in
the past, present, and future?

WHEN YOU'RE AROUND ME, YOU'RE GOING TO GET GLITTER ON YOU.

— Kesha, singer

TIME TO SHINE

Week 19

Beautiful Thing: _____ # _____

Write your **bio.**
Summarize who you **are** and what
you **do** in a way that would make
someone want to meet **you.**

I REALLY HOPE
I CAN MAKE A
DIFFERENCE,
EVEN IN THE
SMALLEST WAY.
I'M LOOKING
FORWARD TO HELPING
AS MUCH AS
I CAN.

— Kate Middleton, princess

BARE NECESSITIES

Week 20

Beautiful Thing: _____ # _____

What are five things you and your
community can't live without?
What are five small things you could
do that would **impact** your community?

IF YOUR DREAM IS ONLY ABOUT YOU, IT'S TOO SMALL.

— Ava DuVernay, director

NATURAL ELEMENTS

Week 21

SPIRITUALITY

Go **outside.**

What do you see in **nature**

that **inspires** you?

HOW YOU HAVE YOUR MIND-SET, IS THE BASE OF WHAT YOU ARE GOING TO GET IN THE FUTURE.

— Valeriya Solovyeva,
tennis professional

GOOD THINGS

SPIRITUALITY

Describe what having a positive
mind-set means to you. What are three **good**
things you can **focus** on every day?

I KNEW I WANTED TO BE AN ASTRONAUT. NOTHING CAN STOP ME.

— Alia Al Mansoori,
aspiring astronaut

BE INSPIRED

Week 23

Beautiful Thing: _____ # _____

Find your **flow** state.
When have you been so **absorbed** in an
activity that you **lost** track of time?

EMPOWERING OUR COLLECTIVE TRIBE AND OWNING OUR INNATE #GIRLPOWER IS WHAT WILL PUSH US THROUGH THESE FRUSTRATING AND DIFFICULT TIMES.

— Haile Thomas,
youngest certified health coach

GET CENTERED

Week 24

Beautiful Thing: _____ # _____

How can you use **spirituality** to get
through a **challenging** situation?

I BELIEVE I'M A UNICORN. UNICORNS ARE VERY MAGICAL AND POWERFUL AND STRONG.

— Justine Skye, musician

BE MAGICAL

Week 25

SPIRITUALITY

What area of your life could use
a little more **magic?** What's one thing you
can do to add a little **sparkle?**

IT'S AN INTERESTING STORY BECAUSE OF MY AGE, BUT IT'S A MOVEMENT OF THOUSANDS, AND I WANT TO EMPHASIZE IT ISN'T ABOUT ONE PERSON.

— Hebh Jamal, youth activist

COLLECTIVELY STRONG

Week 26

SPIRITUALITY

How can you **inspire** your girl tribe
to participate in a **movement?**

STRENGTH

Has fear ever stopped you from doing something you really wanted to do?
Maybe you didn't try out for a team, run for student council, or participate in
an activity because you were afraid of failure. Or maybe you didn't stand up to a
bully or defend a friend who was being mistreated. Everyone has experienced those
butterfly feelings that prevent them from facing a challenge head-on.

Inner strength is what helps you push through those feelings and kick fear in
the butt. It's like a muscle. The more you use it, the stronger it will become. When
you power through a difficult situation, you will feel amazing because you had the
courage to do it.

Strength is not just about bravery. It's about confidence and leadership.
It feels good to stand up for what you believe in. Try something that scares you,
or solve a problem.

You are developing strength when you express yourself to a friend; you
might tell them a secret, communicate your true feelings, or share your hopes and
dreams. These are all strength-builders. Keep doing this even if someone lets you
down. These acts of confiding will help you grow into a person who knows how to
develop strong relationships.

For these next 13 weeks, let yourself ROAR. **It's your time to express yourself
and let your true self shine.** So many exciting things are waiting for you — if
you don't hold yourself back. Your ME Movement is waiting for you to claim it.
Get ready to shout it to the world.

△△△

TEST YOUR STRENGTH IQ

Answer True or False for the following:

- I can leave my comfort zone to try something new. ☐ **T** ☐ **F**

- I can stand up to peer pressure. ☐ **T** ☐ **F**

- I stick with things I love to do even when I have a setback. ☐ **T** ☐ **F**

- I feel great when I try my hardest regardless of the outcome. ☐ **T** ☐ **F**

- I speak up when I see an injustice. ☐ **T** ☐ **F**

- I can try out for a school activity even if it scares me. ☐ **T** ☐ **F**

- I have an awesome group of friends and we support each other. ☐ **T** ☐ **F**

- I can admit when I need help. ☐ **T** ☐ **F**

- I have a strong connection to a mentor, teacher, or supportive adult. ☐ **T** ☐ **F**

- I surround myself with people who cheer me on. ☐ **T** ☐ **F**

Ready to flex those fear-fighting muscles? Add up your "true" answers and give yourself a minute to embrace your STRENGTH. Face your "false" answers head-on and create a plan to make them come true. Use the activities for the next 13 weeks to help you get there.

BE YOURSELF

IF THERE'S ANY DEFINITION TO BEING PERFECT, YOU'RE PERFECT AT BEING YOURSELF.

— Zendaya, actress

What does it mean to you for a
person to **"have it all"** or **"be perfect"**?

EMPOWER YOURSELF

I FEEL CONFIDENT, I FEEL EMPOWERED, I FEEL IN CONTROL.

— Selena Gomez, singer

If you were guaranteed **success,**
what types of things would you **choose** to do?
How would you **empower** yourself?

Beautiful Thing: _____ # _____

PUSH PAST FEAR

WONDER WOMAN IS A FIGHTER, BETTER THAN MOST, BUT IT'S WHAT SHE FIGHTS FOR THAT IS IMPORTANT.

— Gal Gadot, actress

What thoughts, fears, and activities
put **butterflies** in your stomach?
How could you **fight** through your **fears?**

Beautiful Thing: _____ # _____

KINDNESS MATTERS

WHEN I'M DOWN, I TALK TO MYSELF A LOT. I LOOK CRAZY BECAUSE I'M CONSTANTLY HAVING AN ARGUMENT WITH MYSELF.

— Serena Williams,
tennis professional

Be your own best **friend.**
Describe a time when you were particularly
hard on yourself and should have been **kinder.**

Beautiful Thing: _____ # _____

GET GRITTY

TO FALL
DOESN'T MEAN
THAT YOU ARE NOT
GOOD ENOUGH.
YOU HAVE TO
STAND UP AND
TRY HARDER.

— Yusra Mardini, Olympian
and U.N. goodwill ambassador

Remember a time when you **failed** at something.
What did you **learn?**

Beautiful Thing: _____ # _____

BOLD CHOICES

I'M VERY MUCH
A RISK TAKER.
I DON'T HAVE
EXPERIENCE ON MY
SIDE, BUT I HAVE
PERSISTENCE.

— Tyler Haney, founder,
Outdoor Voices

Have you ever taken a **risk** or wish you had?

WRITE IT DOWN

REALLY, IT'S THE STORIES THAT UNITE US, RIGHT? IT'S THOSE HUMAN EXPERIENCES THAT WE ALL SHARE THAT REALLY BRING US TOGETHER.

— Amani Al-Khatahtbeh,
founder, MuslimGirl

Write a letter to your **fifth-grade** self.
What **advice** and words of **wisdom** would you
share about what's coming next in your life?

Beautiful Thing: _____ # _____

FORGE AHEAD

I LOVE GETTING TOLD NO 'CAUSE THEN I FIGHT EVEN MORE.

— Chloë Grace Moretz, actress

Have you ever been told "no"?

How did you **push** through to become a **leader?**

Beautiful Thing: _____ # _____

GET COMFORTABLE

IN THE MADNESS, YOU HAVE TO FIND CALM.

— Lupita Nyong'o, actress

What objects, people, and activities
bring you the greatest **comfort?**

Beautiful Thing: _____ # _____

STAY STRONG

GO AHEAD AND BELIEVE THAT NO ONE SHINES BRIGHTER THAN YOU. BECOME AMAZING, AND BE HAPPY.

—Demi Lovato, singer

What do you **love** most about yourself?

What do you think makes you **shine** "bright"?

Beautiful Thing: _____ # _____

BE BRAVE

GOOD LUCK DRAGGING ME INTO A HORROR MOVIE! I GET SO SCARED. IT'S AN OVERACTIVE IMAGINATION OR SOMETHING.

— Natalia Dyer, actress

What thoughts or **activities** put
your **imagination** into overdrive?

EVEN STRONGER

I WOULD JUST SAY THAT HUMAN BEINGS ARE STRONGER TOGETHER. RELYING ON SOMEONE ELSE IS NOT A SIGN OF WEAKNESS; IT SHOWS STRENGH THAT YOU'RE ABLE TO ACCEPT THAT YOU NEED HELP.

— Dove Cameron, actress

When have you asked for **help?**
How did it feel to let someone **lend** a hand?

Beautiful Thing: _____ # _____

GET PHYSICAL

I DON'T LISTEN TO NAYSAYERS. I KNOW THAT IF I HAVE MY EYE ON MY GOALS AND DREAMS, I WILL BE SUCCESSFUL.

— Gabrielle Jordan Williams,
youth entrepreneur

What **physical** activities make
you feel **powerful?**

STRENGTH

Beautiful Thing: _____ # _____

Have you ever gotten super fired-up and excited about a project or activity?
Maybe you were raising money for a charity, buying your mom a really cool present, or helping a friend out with a problem. Or maybe you were getting prepared for a new school year, starting a new activity, or trying something for the first time. I'm sure you can come up with a hundred examples of meaningful moments in your life.

What brings meaning to your life has nothing to do with some lifelong mission. It's about what's important to you right now. It's your WHY or the reason you do what you do. Your purpose is fun and motivating because it's your plan and not someone else's idea of what you should be doing.

Your purpose doesn't have to be about only one thing. In fact, it's better to value, love, and cherish many things in your life. Your purpose drives you to make good choices, build confidence, and feel passionate in many areas of your life.

You are living your purpose when you identify the most important things in your life and spend time nurturing them. For example, do you love your dog more than anything in the world? Then playing and cuddling together brings meaning to both of your lives. If you want to turn that feeling into something bigger, then you may find your purpose in volunteering at an animal shelter. Both activities are purposeful; one is just bigger than the other.

For the next 13 weeks, start building a list of things that give your life meaning. Fill it with both big and small activities. You will find the most powerful ME Movement comes when you are able to **make a connection between the actions you take and how great they make you feel.**

TEST YOUR PURPOSE IQ

Answer True or False for the following:

- I've created a vision board. ☐ T ☐ F

- I am curious about a lot of different things. ☐ T ☐ F

- I have a social cause that I'm really passionate about. ☐ T ☐ F

- I find ways to make my school projects meaningful to me. ☐ T ☐ F

- I will do something I love even if my friends aren't into it. ☐ T ☐ F

- I have a sibling, friend, or pet who counts on me. ☐ T ☐ F

- I only set goals or resolutions that are important to me. ☐ T ☐ F

- I know that my purpose right now can change later. ☐ T ☐ F

- I have activities, friends, and interests that make me feel awesome. ☐ T ☐ F

Let's add it up! Your "true" answers represent the areas of your life where you experience true meaning. Wouldn't it be amazing to feel that way about everything you do? For the next 13 weeks, think about what you do on a daily basis and how it makes you feel.

I THINK THE BIGGEST PART ABOUT BEING A GIRL BOSS IN THE OFFICE, AT HOME, OR ANYWHERE YOU GO IS JUST KNOWING YOUR VALUE.

— Meghan Markle, princess

#GIRLBOSS

Week 40

Beautiful Thing: _____ # _____

If you could start a **business** right now,
what would it **be?**

I GUESS I THINK ABOUT DOING STUFF THAT NO ONE ELSE HAS DONE.

— Lena Dunham,
actress and writer

LAY THE GROUNDWORK

Week 41

It's time to **plant** your garden.
What seed can you plant **today** that will
grow into something big **tomorrow?**

FINDING BALLET WAS LIKE FINDING THIS MISSING PIECE OF MYSELF.

— Misty Copeland, ballet dancer

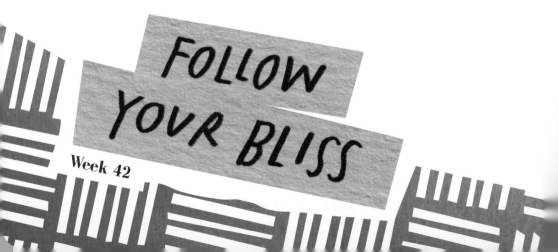

FOLLOW YOUR BLISS

Week 42

Beautiful Thing: _____ # _____

What **hobbies** do you get **lost** doing?
Have you found any hobbies that
make you feel **complete?**

YOU CAN HAVE
AN "IT" MOMENT,
BUT YOU HAVE TO
KNOW HOW TO
CONTINUE TO
MOVE THIS
MOVEMENT INTO
SOMETHING THAT'S
BIGGER THAN
YOURSELF.

— Ashley Graham, model

BE INVOLVED

Week 43

What can you do to
participate in the social causes
that get you most **fired up?**

YOU CAN DO
ANYTHING AND
BE A STAR.
YOU CAN DRESS
LIKE WHOEVER
YOU WANT, AND
YOU CAN DO
WHATEVER
YOU WANT.

— Alessia Cara, singer

LOOKING UP

Week 44

Who are the **role models** in your
life that **inspire** you to be whoever
and whatever you want to be?

SO EVERYWHERE THAT I AM, I LIKE TO KEEP AN OPEN MIND AND JUST GET IDEAS FROM EVERYTHING.

— Bethany Mota, internet star

MEANINGFUL IDEAS

Week 45

Create four new **holidays** based on dates
that mean something to **you.**

I BELIEVE YOU
CAN ACCOMPLISH
YOUR DREAMS
NO MATTER HOW
OLD YOU ARE.
I'M DOING IT!

— WondaGurl, producer

LEAD BY EXAMPLE

Week 46

Beautiful Thing: _____ # _____

Go online and find five youth who are
out there **pursuing** their **dreams** right now.
What can you **learn** from them?

WHATEVER HAPPENS I JUST DON'T WANT TO QUIT DOING THIS.

—Eefje "Sjokz" Depoortere,
eSports host

MY AMAZING YEAR

Week 47

Beautiful Thing: _____ # _____

What is the most **incredible** thing that
has happened to **you** this year?

I DON'T WANT
TO BE REMEMBERED
AS THE GIRL WHO
WAS SHOT.
I WANT TO BE
REMEMBERED AS
THE GIRL WHO
STOOD UP.

— Malala Yousafzai, activist

BRIGHT FUTURE

Week 48

Beautiful Thing: _____ # _____

Close your eyes and **visualize** all of
your **dreams** coming true. What would
you like to be **remembered** as?

I'M A ROLLER COASTER THAT ONLY GOES UP.

—Autumn de Forest, art prodigy

SHARE THE WEALTH

Week 49

Beautiful Thing: _____ # _____

Dig deeper into a subject that **interests** you.
How can you **share** what
you've **learned** with another person?

I HAVE BEEN
ABLE TO FIND
BALANCE IN
EVERYTHING I AM
INVOLVED IN
BECAUSE I TRULY
BELIEVE IN ALL
THAT I DO.

— Nadya Okamoto, activist

BE PRODUCTIVE

Week 50

Beautiful Thing: _____ # _____

Set a 30-day **goal.**
Write down all of the **steps** you need
to complete in order to **achieve** it.

NEVER LET ANYONE TELL YOU THAT YOU CAN'T CHANGE THE WORLD BECAUSE YOU CAN.

— Mari Copeny, youth activist

RISING UP

Week 51

Beautiful Thing: _____ # _____

When have you been **told**
you couldn't **achieve** something,
but you **conquered** it anyway?

NEVER SAY NO TO ANYTHING, WHATEVER THE UNIVERSE BRINGS ME. I'VE ALWAYS LIVED BY THAT.

— Ruby Rose, actress

A LIFE IN HARMONY

Week 52

Beautiful Thing: _____ # _____

What does it mean to **live**
an **abundant** life?

Ideas to **Inspire** Me

Ideas to **Inspire** Me

Ideas to **Inspire** Me

Ideas to **Inspire** Me

Ideas to **Inspire** Me

Ideas to **Inspire** Me